MAGELLAN

—Other titles in the Great Explorers of the World series—

COLUMBUS
Opening Up
the New World
ISBN-13: 978-1-59845-101-6
ISBN-10:　　1-59845-101-4

LA SALLE
French Explorer
of the Mississippi
ISBN-13: 978-1-59845-098-9
ISBN-10:　　1-59845-098-0

HENRY HUDSON
Discoverer of the Hudson River
ISBN-13: 978-1-59845-123-8
ISBN-10:　　1-59845-123-5

MAGELLAN
First to Circle the Globe
ISBN-13: 978-1-59845-097-2
ISBN-10:　　1-59845-097-2

HERNANDO DE SOTO
Spanish Conquistador
in the Americas
ISBN-13: 978-1-59845-104-7
ISBN-10:　　1-59845-104-9

MARCO POLO
Amazing Adventures
in China
ISBN-13: 978-1-59845-103-0
ISBN-10:　　1-59845-103-0

MAGELLAN

Great Explorers of the World

First to Circle the Globe

David Aretha

Enslow Publishers, Inc.
40 Industrial Road
Box 398
Berkeley Heights, NJ 07922
USA
http://www.enslow.com

Library of Congress Cataloging-in-Publication Data

Aretha, David.
  Magellan : first to circle the globe / David Aretha.
      p. cm. — (Great explorers of the world)
  Includes bibliographical references and index.
  Summary: "Explores Ferdinand Magellan's life from his childhood to his travels to his death, his
discoveries and accomplishments, and his impact on world history"—Provided by publisher.
  ISBN-13: 978-1-59845-097-2 (hardcover)
  ISBN-10: 1-59845-097-2 (hardcover)
  1. Magalhães, Fernão de, d. 1521. 2. Explorers—Portugal—Biography. 3. Voyages around the
world—Juvenile literature. I. Title.
  G286.M2A86 2009
  910.4'1—dc22
  [B]
                                    2008013550

Printed in the United States of America

10 9 8 7 6 5 4 3 2 1

To Our Readers: We have done our best to make sure all Internet Addresses in this book were active and
appropriate when we went to press. However, the author and the publisher have no control over and assume
no liability for the material available on those Internet sites or on other Web sites they may link to. Any com-
ments or suggestions can be sent by e-mail to comments@enslow.com or to the address on the back cover.

♻ Enslow Publishers, Inc., is committed to printing our books on recycled paper. The paper in every book
contains 10% to 30% post-consumer waste (PCW). The cover board on the outside of each book contains 100%
PCW. Our goal is to do our part to help young people and the environment too!

Photo Credits: © Corel Corporation, pp. 54–55, 62; DigitalVision, pp. 12, 58–59; Enslow Publishers, Inc.,
p. 35; The Granger Collection, New York, pp. 50, 65, 95; © 2008 JupiterImages Corporation, p. 10; Library of
Congress, pp. 20, 46; Public domain image, pp. 16–17, 24, 77; Public domain image via Wikipedia.org,
pp. 83, 89, 92, 101; NASA, p. 78; Shutterstock®, pp. 42–43, 71, 73, 86–87, 103.

Ship Illustration Used in Chapter Openers: Dover Publications, Inc.

Cover Illustration: Library of Congress (portrait of Ferdinand Magellan).

Contents

EXPLORER TIMELINE

1480 — Magellan is likely born during this year, in Portugal.

1488 — Portugal's Bartolomeu Dias becomes the first European to sail around the southern tip of Africa.

1492 — Sailing for Spain, Christopher Columbus lands in America; he mistakenly thinks he has reached Asia.

— Magellan becomes a page in Portugal's royal court.

1494 — Spain and Portugal sign the Treaty of Tordesillas; lands east of an agreed-upon line will be under the domain of Portugal, and lands west will belong to Spain.

1498 — Portugal's Vasco da Gama reaches India after sailing around Africa.

1505 — Magellan sails on his first expedition, bound for Africa and then India.

1509 — Is wounded in battle against Indians and Arabs on the island of Diu.

— Proves heroic in battle in Malacca.

1511 — Serves as a ship captain for the first time, in a return voyage to Malacca.

1513 — Goes to Morocco, where he is wounded in battle.

1516 — Portugal's King Manuel dismisses Magellan's requests for a pay raise or command of a ship.

1517 — Magellan moves to Spain, gets married, and builds an alliance with Spanish power brokers.

1518 — Convinces King Charles I of Spain that he can reach the Orient's Spice Islands by sailing through a passageway in South America; the king agrees to sponsor the voyage.

1519 — *September:* Magellan's fleet of five ships departs Spain for the westward trip to the Spice Islands.

— *December:* The fleet arrives at Rio de Janeiro, Brazil.

1520 — *March-August:* The fleet winters at San Julián, Argentina; Magellan ingeniously avoids mutiny in April.

— *October:* Magellan's fleet discovers *el paso*, the passageway through southern South America.

— *November 28:* The fleet begins its voyage across the Pacific Ocean, during which sailors will die from hunger, thirst, heat, and disease.

1521 — *March 6:* The fleet reaches the island of Guam, where the sailors stock up on much needed food and water.

— *Late March:* The fleet reaches the Malay Peninsula in Asia; Magellan and his crew become the first-known people to sail west to Asia, and therefore prove that the world is round.

— *April:* The crew stays on the island of Cebu; the fleet's priests baptize thousands of Cebu natives and those on nearby islands.

— *April 27:* Magellan dies in battle on the island of Mactan.

— *May 1:* Humabon, king of Cebu, orchestrates the murder of twenty-seven fleet members.

— *November 8:* The fleet, now down to two ships, finally reaches the Spice Islands.

1522 — *September 8:* Eighteen members of the fleet (along with three Moluccan islanders) reach Seville, Spain, becoming the first-known people to sail around the world.

Chapter 1

THE HUMILIATION

It was 1513, and Ferdinand Magellan was down on his luck. After eight years in Asia, he had just returned to his native Portugal. Magellan, thirty-three years old, had enjoyed privilege and success throughout his life. The son of Portuguese aristocrats, he had been educated at the royal court. He had learned his lessons well, and he had become a masterful navigator and astronomer. Magellan had sailed to Asia, then known as the Orient—land of riches—and in 1511 even captained his own ship. He had served on the first Portuguese ship ever to sail to the Philippines.

Portugal's King Manuel had become very wealthy from the services of Magellan and other brave sailors. But the king did not reward seamen for their great service to Portugal—as Magellan was finding out. When he visited the royal palace in 1513, he learned that he still held the lowly rank of junior squire.

King Manuel was not about to do any favors for Ferdinand Magellan; their families had a long-established rivalry. Portugal's previous ruler, King John II, had personally killed Manuel's brother.

This 1695 Flemish woodcut depicts Magellan.

Magellan's family strongly supported King John II, and so Manuel had long disliked Ferdinand Magellan.[1] In fact, Magellan discovered upon his trip to the palace that his small salary from the king had been cut in half. Manuel also refused Magellan's request to sail on Portugal's next sea voyage.

Manuel permitted Magellan to serve in North Africa, where the Portuguese were fighting against Arabs. Amid hostilities, a spear struck Magellan in the right knee. When he returned to Portugal in 1516, he still walked with a limp. His income remained pitifully small, and his valuable Asian goods had been stolen. Magellan was so desperate that he bribed a royal usher for a brief meeting with the king.

King Manuel granted the request, and Magellan knelt before him while surrounded by members of the royal court. Swallowing his pride, Magellan asked for a modest raise in pay based on his many years of service to Portugal. Revealing his contempt for his visitor, the king quickly denied the request. Magellan, former captain of his own ship, then asked if he could command a royal caravel (ship)—or even a privately owned ship. Manuel flatly refused both requests.

Returning the contempt, Magellan boldly asked if he could serve another king. Manuel responded that Magellan could do as he pleased, for his service mattered little to him. According to

Portuguese custom, visitors were expected to kiss the king's hand after meeting with him. Despite his humiliating encounter with King Manuel, Magellan attempted the humble gesture. But the king insulted his visitor even further by pulling his hand away. Ashamed, Magellan hobbled away.

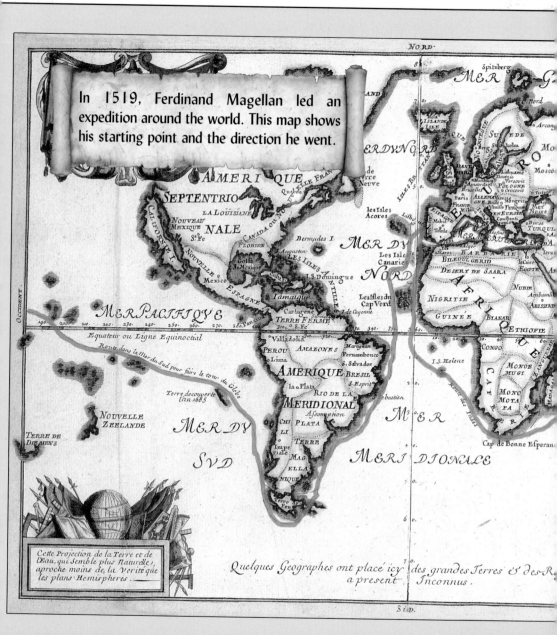

In 1519, Ferdinand Magellan led an expedition around the world. This map shows his starting point and the direction he went.

Magellan would rise above this disgrace. He would convince the Spanish king to grant him command of a historic expedition. Magellan and his fleet would try to become the first to reach Asia by going west. Magellan would prove to be an extraordinary captain. He would ingeniously avoid mutiny and fight off enemy attackers. More amazingly, he would endure a death-defying, seemingly endless journey across an unknown body of water—one he would name the Pacific Ocean. Part of his fleet would sail all the way back to Spain.

The vain King Manuel would become a minor figure in history. But the lowly junior squire with the pitiful limp would live in immortality. We will forever recognize Ferdinand Magellan for leading the first success-ful attempt to sail around the world.

Chapter 2

The Quest for Cheaper Pepper

What motivated Europeans to sail thousands of miles to Asia? You know the answer. It's on the tip of your tongue: taste buds. "Lacking spices," wrote historian Stefan Zweig, "the food of Northern Europe was unspeakably monotonous and insipid."[1]

In the 1400s, when Ferdinand Magellan was born, such European countries as Spain, Portugal, France, and England lacked tasty foods. They could not produce sugar and lemons (sweet and sour). And although salt was plentiful, pepper was not. Pepper not only added much needed flavor, but it was used (along with salt) to prevent meat from going bad.

The Spice Islands (present-day Indonesia) in Southeast Asia had an abundance of pepper and other spices that the Western world craved. What a Spaniard would not give for a pinch of cinnamon, a dash of nutmeg, or a taste of ginger! European women longed for the perfumes of the Orient, while Catholic churches wanted incense for religious services. In addition, wealthy Europeans were willing to pay big money for silks from China, pearls from

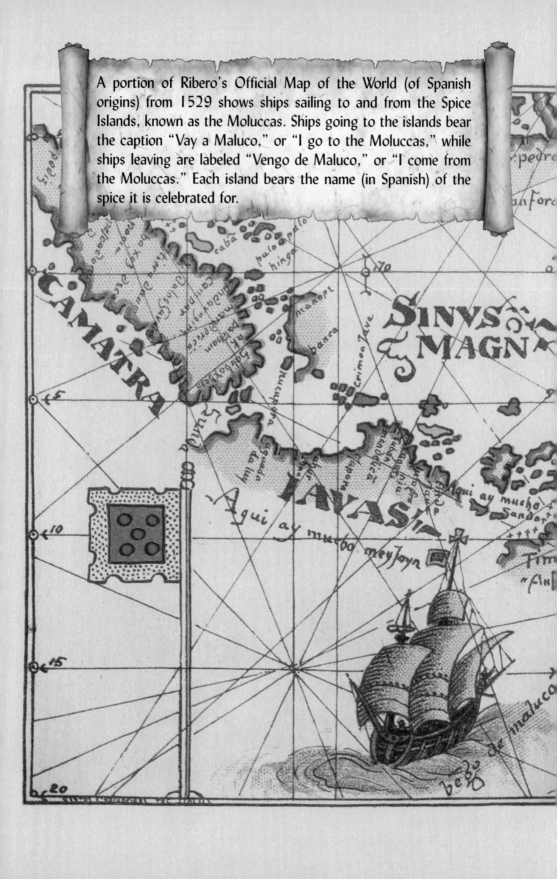

A portion of Ribero's Official Map of the World (of Spanish origins) from 1529 shows ships sailing to and from the Spice Islands, known as the Moluccas. Ships going to the islands bear the caption "Vay a Maluco," or "I go to the Moluccas," while ships leaving are labeled "Vengo de Maluco," or "I come from the Moluccas." Each island bears the name (in Spanish) of the spice it is celebrated for.

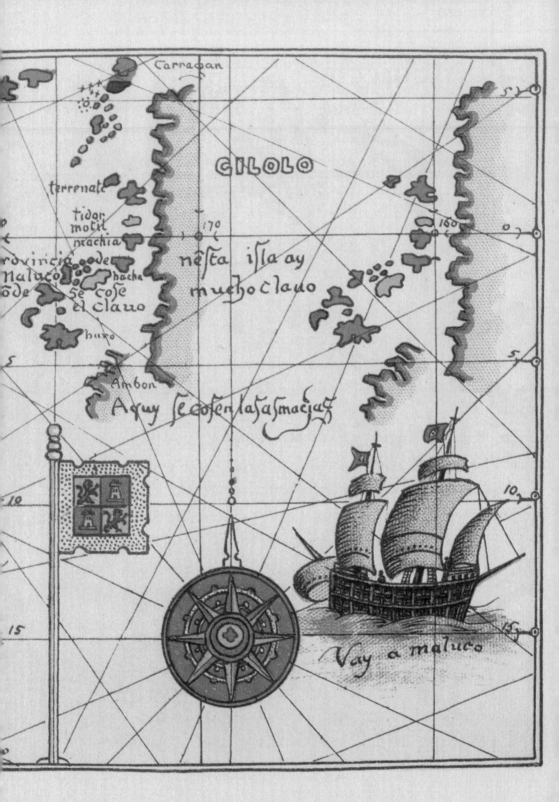

Ceylon (present-day Sri Lanka), and diamonds from Hindustan (present-day India).

THE HIGH PRICE OF PEPPER

While most of the Orient's treasures were luxuries, Europeans considered pepper a necessity. Unfortunately, in the 1400s, it was extremely expensive. That was because the trade route from the Orient to Europe was dominated by merchants. Each of them made money when spices passed through their hands.

It took many weeks for a sack of pepper to make it from the Spice Islands to western Europe. First, Asian ships lugged it to the Malay Peninsula. There, merchants had to pay the prince for the right to transfer the cargo to a larger ship. The sack then was shipped across the Bay of Bengal to India. Other ships transported it along the coast of India to the Arabian Sea. It then traveled across that great body of water to the Persian Gulf. All the while, storms and pirates threatened the crew and cargo. At each stop, traders were forced to pay local taxes.

The sack of pepper still had a long way to go to reach its destination. Camel drivers made the slow, parched trip across the Arabian Desert. Eventually, the sack of pepper reached the Mediterranean Sea, where it was sold to traders. These men hauled the pepper to the Western

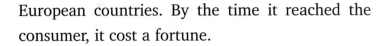

European countries. By the time it reached the consumer, it cost a fortune.

THE SEARCH FOR A BETTER ROUTE

For many years, western Europeans sought a cheaper route to the Orient—one that avoided the heavy taxation by foreigners. The best way would be to sail all the way to the Spice Islands, but no ship had ever sailed that far. In the mid-1400s, Portugal took the lead in transoceanic travel.

At Sagres, a town in southern Portugal, Prince Henry established a center for the study of astronomy, navigation, and naval architecture. The Portuguese created a new ship called a caravel. With its sleek hull construction, the caravel was faster and more maneuverable than previous ships had been. Because of this, it was able to explore small bays and narrow rivers. The Portuguese also developed better navigation equipment. Throughout the century, Portuguese captains became more and more adventurous, traveling farther south on the Atlantic.

In 1434, Portuguese captain Gil Eannes sailed south of Cape Bojador on the northwest coast of Africa. His journey disproved the myth that sea monsters or boiling waters lay south of that area. With further naval improvements, explorers sailed farther south along Africa's western coast. In

1488, Bartolomeu Dias became the first to round the southern tip of the African continent. Dias's breakthrough excited Portugal's King John II, who wanted to keep pushing eastward.

In 1498, after King John's death, Vasco da Gama achieved the great dream. He sailed around

Christopher Columbus set sail on his first voyage to the Americas on August 3, 1492.

Africa and all the way to India, where he took spices on board. In succeeding years, the Portuguese would transport large quantities of spices and other Asian riches back to the home country. Portugal, along with the neighboring country of Spain, became one of the two leading powers in western Europe.

Earlier in the 1490s, King John had turned down Christopher Columbus's plan for a western route to Asia. Columbus went to Spain, which sponsored his fabled journey. In 1492, Columbus thought he had reached Asia by heading west across the Atlantic. In reality, he had reached the Americas. The only way to reach Asia by going west was to cross the Atlantic and then the enormous Pacific Ocean. But no one knew that at the time. In fact, the Pacific had not been discovered by Europeans yet, and no one had any idea that it stretched more than ten thousand miles wide.

Years would pass before any European would lead a western voyage around the globe. The first man to attempt such an adventure would be Ferdinand Magellan.

Chapter 3

Growing Up in the Royal Court

The exact details of Ferdinand Magellan's youth remain a mystery. Historians do not know for sure what year he was born, although the spring of 1480 is the best guess. In different countries, he is known by different names. Ferdinand Magellan is the English version, but in Portuguese his name is Fernão de Magalhães. Spanish-speaking people call him Fernando (or Hernando) de Magallanes.

Historians once thought that Magellan was born in the village of Sabrosa, Portugal. Evidence indicates, however, that the nearby town of Oporto may have been his birthplace. Ferdinand is believed to have been the third child of Pedro Magalhães and Alda de Mezquita Pimenta. He grew up on a farm with Diego, his brother, and at least two sisters.

Ferdinand and his family lived in a most unusual home—the remnants of an old watchtower. The first floor housed farm animals, while the Magellans lived upstairs. Historians have offered many speculations about Ferdinand's childhood: as a boy, he crushed grapes with his feet to help his father make wine. He shot small animals with a crossbow for

Magellan

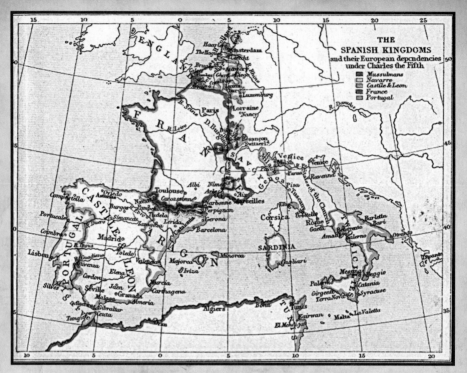

This map shows the Spanish kingdoms under Charles the Fifth, Holy Roman Emperor from 1519 to 1556, who was also known as Charles I of Spain. Portugal's capital city of Lisbon, where Magellan studied at the royal court, is shown at the lower left.

food, and he attended church and holiday feasts. And he danced with family members in the evenings under the glow of torchlight.

Due to the harsh winters and the demanding chores required of farm families, Ferdinand developed the strong work ethic that would contribute to his later successes. He also strongly adhered to his Christian faith.

24

☻ Off to the Royal Court

If the Magellan family members had been mere commoners, Ferdinand's name would have been lost to history. But they happened to be members of Portugal's minor nobility. As such, Diego and Ferdinand were allowed to be educated at the royal court in Portugal's capital city of Lisbon. The two brothers attended the school for pages. In exchange for running errands for King John II's royal court, the pages received an education superior to that of most Portuguese.

In school, Ferdinand learned such skills as hunting, jousting, and sword fighting. He also learned much about sea travel in the school founded by Prince Henry the Navigator at Sagres. Experienced seamen taught at the school, and Ferdinand learned geometry, mapmaking, astronomy, and celestial navigation. The more he learned, the more he desired to test his skills on a great adventure.

While Ferdinand attended school, Duke Manuel supervised all the pages. Manuel was the brother of Queen Leonor. He was also related to the Braganza family, a rival to Portugal's ruling royal family. Duke Manuel never liked Ferdinand, perhaps because the Magellan family was loyal to King John II. Should the king (who had no sons) die, Manuel would inherit the throne.

COLVMBVS'S DISCOVERY

Nautical excitement filled the air in 1493. Italian sailor Christopher Columbus, while sailing under the Spanish flag, landed in a Portuguese harbor due to a storm. Columbus told King John II that he had reached Asia by traveling west across the Atlantic. As proof, Columbus showed the king a few men—kidnapped by his crew—who looked like Asians. They were really natives of America, but the Europeans did not realize it at the time. The body of land that Columbus "discovered" was simply called the New World.

After Columbus's discovery, Portugal's King John wanted to make future explorations favorable for his country. To that end, he initiated the signing of the Treaty of Tordesillas on June 7, 1494. The treaty (between Spain and Portugal) established the zones of influence for each country. According to the treaty, all land discovered west of (what we know today as) 46°37'W would fall under Spain's control.[1] Portugal would have entitlement to new lands east of that line. This demarcation line lay several hundred miles east of North America's East Coast.

Fortunately for King John, the Orient (and all its riches) lay within Portugal's domain. After the treaty was signed, the king began preparations for two voyages to India—a land that neither Portugal nor Spain had yet reached. One expedition would head east and the other west. Tragically, the plan never materialized. In October 1495, assassins are thought to have fatally poisoned King John. The Braganzas became Portugal's new royal family, and Duke Manuel became King Manuel I.

KING MANUEL RULES

Manuel's ascension sent shock waves through Portugal. He took the property of those who had been loyal to King John. Portuguese Jews had to either be baptized as Christians or face banishment or death. The school for pages, which included Ferdinand Magellan, was moved to Manuel's royal court.

At first, Manuel showed little interest in explorations of the East. Only when Spanish pepper merchants started to infringe on Portuguese trade did Manuel become interested in establishing a sea route to India. In 1497, King Manuel commissioned Vasco da Gama to lead a fleet of four ships eastward to India. At the time of this historic launch, Magellan worked in the king's palace as a clerk for the naval department.

After a harrowing journey, da Gama returned to Portugal on September 9, 1499. Although only 54 members of the original crew of 170 survived, da Gama did return with precious spices. The success inspired Manuel to send many more ships eastward to India. They returned with more fortunes, making Portugal's nobility and merchants rich.

Becoming as ambitious as his predecessor, King Manuel in 1501 sent three fleets to find a western route to Asia. Italian Amerigo Vespucci was a member of one fleet and helped to chart and navigate; Goncalo Coelho served as commander. Like Christopher Columbus, Vespucci discovered land. But unlike Columbus, Vespucci did not believe it was Asia. He said it was a different continent, and he was right; he had reached Brazil. In 1507, Martin Waldseemüller of Germany would create a map and name the new continent America.

Vespucci kept traveling south along the Brazilian coast, hoping to find a passageway that led further west. Failing in this attempt, he returned home. For nearly two decades, Portuguese explorers would attempt to find *el paso*—the passageway in southern South America that would lead to the other side of the New World.

India House

Early in the 1500s, Magellan wanted to be among the many Portuguese men who were sailing east to Asia. However, he was denied this opportunity because of King Manuel's dislike for him. Magellan instead worked in Lisbon at India House, which collected taxes on imports and exports. The work may have been dull, but Ferdinand found much to keep his interest. At India House, he had access to the Portuguese explorers' ship logs, maps, and reports of discoveries. He also listened in on meetings by the country's top navigators and scientists. Absorbing all that he could, Magellan became an expert himself on navigation. If only he could put his skills to practice.

🌐 MAGELLAN'S BIG BREAK

In 1505, Magellan's chance for adventure finally arrived. King Manuel wanted to send a large expedition to the east coast of Africa and the west coast of India. The king's goal was to control the trade routes in the Indian Ocean, between Europe and India. To this end, the fleet members would destroy Arab trading stations and build Portuguese forts and naval bases.

Francisco de Almeida, Portugal's viceroy of India, would captain the fleet. Almeida asked that members of India House accompany him. Not only did Ferdinand get to go, but so did his brother, Diego. The day of launch—the biggest moment yet of Magellan's life—was set for March 25, 1505.

Chapter 4

Gentleman Adventurer

AS he prepared to sail on that early spring morning in 1505, Magellan must have realized that he might never return. Many people had died on voyages to Asia. Violent storms, diseases, and battles with enemies killed many Portuguese sailors.

Francisco de Almeida's fleet of twenty-two ships—including fourteen carracks and six caravels—was the largest ever assembled in Portugal's history. Fifteen hundred members of the crew were soldiers, fully equipped and armored. An additional two hundred were bombardiers or gunners. Magellan was among the four hundred "gentlemen adventurers." Working without pay, this group would carry out whatever military or civil duties were requested of them. In addition to the great manpower, the ships carried many tons of timber to build fortresses.

This mission, scheduled to last three years, was extraordinarily ambitious. Almeida, on King Manuel's order, was to completely secure the Portuguese trade route. His troops would seize water passageways, build forts, conquer cities, and set up colonies. The Arab and Indian traders would be eliminated, making the spice trade even more profitable for Portugal. Moreover, Almeida was to spread Christianity in all the territories he conquered.

The mission had the feel of a holy crusade. After attending Mass on March 25, the fleet members marched solemnly to the harbor. A ceremony marked by the explosion of gunfire signaled their farewell.

SECURING THE AFRICAN COAST

In the first leg of the journey, the fleet had to sail around the southern tip of Africa. The farther south they went, the colder it was. Ice formed on the ships, and ferocious waves tossed nine men to their watery death. In late June, the fleet rounded the tip of Africa and sailed northward in the Indian Ocean.

Arab traders on the east coast of Africa had every reason to fear Almeida's fleet. At Kilwa, the Portuguese soldiers killed many Arab men and set buildings on fire. At multiple points along the coast, Almeida deployed soldiers and assigned men to build forts. He replaced hostile leaders with local natives who swore allegiance to the Portuguese king. When a sheik (or Arab chief) at Mombasa resisted takeover, Almeida's men burned down the city.

Not all of the ships continued north. Some, including Magellan's, stayed behind to patrol the coast. Nuno Vaz Pereira, commander of the Portuguese patrol ships, recognized Ferdinand's navigational skills. He promoted Magellan to the position of pilot's assistant. In 1507, when Pereira was ordered to sail to India, Ferdinand Magellan went with him.

ALMEIDA'S RAGE

In 1507 and into 1508, Magellan sailed to Ceylon, an island near southeast India (present-day Sri Lanka). However, an urgent situation required that the ship join Almeida's fleet in the Indian Ocean. Magellan and his shipmates learned that Almeida's son had been killed in battle in Dabul, India. Almeida, in a mad rage, sought revenge. He led his fleet to Dabul and ordered his soldiers to kill every person in the city. They spared no one, not even the children.

Still thirsting for blood, Almeida went after his naval enemy—the Indian and Arab fleet that was somewhere in the Indian Ocean. He found them on the island of Diu, northwest of India, in February 1509. The fleet was ten times the size of Almeida's—two hundred ships and twenty thousand men. Nevertheless, Almeida's troops, Magellan included, attacked. Although the Indians and Arabs retreated, many Portuguese men

died in the savage battle. Captain Pereira was killed, and Magellan was wounded.

ON TO MALACCA

For weeks, Magellan recovered in Cochin, the Portuguese colony in India. Afterward, he served as a knight, protecting Cochin from unfriendly Indians. By summer, he willingly agreed to join another potentially dangerous expedition. King Manuel called for a fleet to sail two thousand miles further east. Their destination: Malacca on the Malay Peninsula, near present-day Singapore.

It was a monumental and bold journey. Malacca was near the fabled Spice Islands, and a tremendous amount of riches passed through the Malacca port. They included pepper and nutmeg as well as gold, rubies, and porcelains. For centuries, Chinese and Arabs had controlled these valuable ports. Now Portuguese troops, including Magellan, were about to invade their territory.

After crossing the Bay of Bengal, the fleet of Captain Diogo Lopes de Sequeira arrived at Malacca on September 11, 1509. The crew must have been awestruck. An enormous number of ships, including those from China and the Middle East, filled the harbor. High walls lined the coast, each topped with brass cannons that pointed toward the sea. Above the mansions and temples

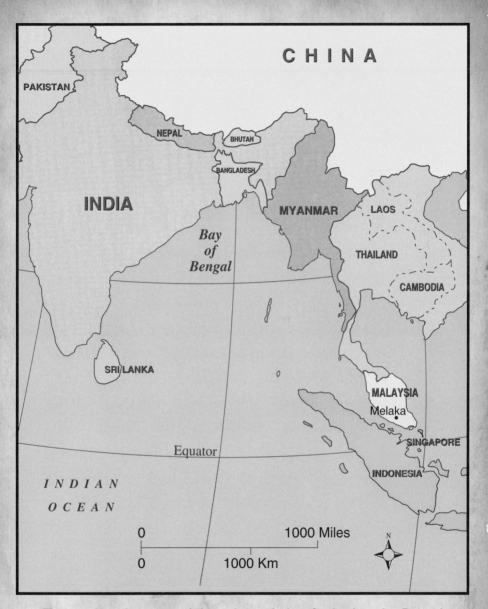

This modern-day map of Asia shows India, Sri Lanka, the Bay of Bengal, the Indian Ocean, Singapore, and Melaka (the modern spelling of "Malacca") in Malaysia. Magellan journeyed to Malacca in September 1509 as part of Almeida's expedition.

of the city stood the palace of Malacca's sultan Mohammed.

THE DEVIOUS SULTAN

At first, Sultan Mohammed was friendly to Captain Sequeira. He even granted the Portuguese permission to open a trading post on the waterfront. However, the goodwill was only a trap. He wanted to lure the Portuguese ships to shore so that he could easily capture them, including their cargo and crew members.

Several days after their arrival, Sequeira played chess on his ship with a Malay nobleman. Meanwhile, the Portuguese sensed danger. Magellan entered Sequeira's cabin and told him that potentially hostile sampans (flat-bottomed Chinese sailboats) surrounded the ship. As the Portuguese reacted in alarm, the sultan's troops attacked. Many of the Portuguese who were on shore were captured. Dozens of others were killed as they tried to fight their way back to the beach.

In the heat of battle, Magellan proved heroic. He and two others jumped from their ship into a small boat and rowed frantically toward the beach. There they captured a large longboat from the Malays. Many Portuguese climbed into the longboat, which headed back to the ships amid hostile sampans. Magellan and his two accomplices had saved the men's lives. Sequeira and his fleet sailed away.

MAGELLAN CAPTAINS A CARAVEL

Though chased out of Malacca, the Portuguese continued their aggression in Asia. Afonso de Albuquerque was now Portugal's viceroy of India. Like other Christian leaders, Albuquerque was troubled by the spread of Islam (the Muslim religion) throughout Asia. He wanted to eliminate Arabs from India, either by driving them out or killing them.

Twice in 1510, Albuquerque's troops attacked Goa, a seaport on India's west coast. The decisive battle took place in November. Over a three-day span, Portuguese soldiers killed more than eight thousand Arabs, sparing not even the children. Magellan was with the fleet that attacked, though he likely did not participate in the slaughter.

That said, Magellan fully supported Portugal's plans for conquest. In March 1511, a fleet prepared to leave Goa for Malacca. Due to his superior maritime skills, Magellan was allowed to captain one of the fleet's nineteen caravels. The Portuguese sought revenge for their 1509 eviction.

When the ships arrived in Malacca, Portuguese soldiers stormed the beaches. With an army of eight hundred soldiers and six hundred archers,

they took on the sultan's army of twenty thousand men. Due to their superior weaponry, the Portuguese troops eventually won a battle that took weeks.

Those Malaccans who surrendered were taken as slaves. Rewarding his captains, Albuquerque informed them that they each could keep a slave for themselves. Magellan selected a boy whom he named Enrique de Malacca. Enrique remained "a loyal and devoted servant until his master's death . . . [and] was to play a significant role in Magellan's great enterprise."[1] Meanwhile, the Portuguese plundered a massive amount of treasures from Malacca. However, when they attempted to haul it on one ship to Goa, the boat sank and the fortune was lost.

STRIPPED OF HIS CAPTAINSHIP

For more than a year, Magellan stayed in Malacca. He served on patrol duty, in command of a ship. All the while, he hungered to see more of his world. When a group of sailors went to explore the eastern waters of the Spice Islands, Magellan went with them, serving as navigator. Little is known about their journey, but historians believe that they probably reached the Philippines.

The Portuguese rulers tolerated murder and plunder, and honesty apparently was not acceptable. Magellan learned that lesson the hard way.

Based on navigational measurements, Magellan concluded that the Spice Islands did not belong to Portugal (according to the parameters set by the Treaty of Tordesillas). Magellan recorded his findings in an official report, which angered King Manuel. Subsequently, Magellan was stripped of his captainship and ordered to return to Portugal.

GOING HOME

In the spring or early summer of 1512, Magellan returned to Lisbon. He had been gone seven years, but it must have seemed like seventy. Lisbon had changed so much. As explained by Magellan biographer Stefan Zweig: "The port was thronged with masts flying the flags of every nation of Europe. . . . Thousands of persons hurried to and fro along the streets which led between rows of newly erected palaces. Every workshop hummed with talk about the conquest of the Indies [Orient]. Lisbon, which had been a petty provincial city, had become one of the great capitals of the world, and the home of luxury."[2]

Manuel had become the richest king in Europe—all because of his daring sailors and soldiers. Yet during what later became known as the Age of Discovery, kings were notorious for ignoring their ocean warriors. King Manuel was no different. Upon visiting the royal palace, Magellan found that he still was listed as a junior

squire. This was the same rank he had held when he left in 1505, seven years earlier. His experience as a captain and navigator, and his heroics in battle, meant nothing to King Manuel.

Injury and Insult

For a year, Magellan performed minor duties for a meager income. Restless, he sought more adventure despite the possibility of danger. In 1513, he agreed to join a military expedition to Morocco (in North Africa) to fight the Arab enemy. Magellan assisted the navigator, John of Lisbon, on the sea voyage to Morocco. Once on land, he had to fight. Magellan engaged in hand-to-hand combat and suffered a serious wound—a lance was thrust into his left knee.

Thus began Magellan's plunge to the lowest depths of his life. Now disabled, he could no longer fight. In Morocco, he served as a quartermaster and looked after the horses, cattle, and sheep. After a dozen sheep vanished one night, Magellan was accused of selling them to the Arabs. Defiant, Magellan sailed back to Portugal to defend himself. As it turned out, King Manuel was more upset that Magellan had left the army without leave. Magellan was cleared of all charges of wrongdoing and was ordered back to Morocco. He returned there briefly, then went back to Lisbon.

When Magellan met the king in 1516, the explorer was facing a crisis. He was about thirty-six years old, nearly broke, and lame. Short and stocky with a bushy black beard, he did not cut the image of a nobleman. He was a quiet man with few friends, but he remained as ambitious as ever.

Magellan's meeting with King Manuel may have been the most humiliating moment of his life. While Magellan kneeled in front of the king like a beggar, the king denied his two requests. Only his third request—"Could he serve another king?"—met with acceptance. His years of service had amounted to nothing. He was of no importance; the king told him so.

Magellan left Lisbon in a hurry. That very evening, he sailed north to Porto, where he would live through the winter. This waterfront city brimmed with former sailors like Magellan. They had served with distinction in the Far East, only to return to cold shoulders in Lisbon. Many drank ale to drown their sorrows, and some talked about switching their allegiance to Spain. Magellan likely considered such a move, but he needed a reason to go. In 1517, he found one.

AN EXCITING IDEA

That year, John of Lisbon met up with Magellan. John informed his friend that he had sailed to the southern coasts of the New World (Brazil). He

Magellan spent the winter of 1516–1517 in Porto, Portugal, after his humiliating meeting with King Manuel. The present-day port is pictured.

believed he had discovered *el paso,* the passageway through the Americas to Asia.

Both men believed that the distance between the Americas and the Spice Islands was not very great. The two dreamed of passing through el paso—an unprecedented accomplishment by Europeans—and reaching the Spice Islands in quick time. Should they discover this long-sought western route to Asia, they would be hailed as heroes.

Just like John of Lisbon, Ferdinand Magellan became excited by the idea of finding el paso. That spring, John helped his friend in a dangerous endeavor. Magellan knew that within the treasury of King Manuel lay a secret map. Magellan once had seen it. The map had been created by a navigator who had sailed southward down the coast of Brazil. The man was

convinced that he had found a water passage through southern South America that led to an ocean on the other side. In the spring of 1517, Magellan entered the king's mapmaking room and copied the map. It confirmed that el paso was where John had said it was.

MAGELLAN'S NEW LIFE

John and Magellan were itching to embark on this voyage of discovery, but they needed the support of a king. Later in 1517, Magellan began to make the right contacts. He joined up with an old sailor friend, Duarte Barbosa. Like Magellan, Barbosa held a grudge against King Manuel. More importantly, Duarte's uncle, Diogo Barbosa, knew Spanish noblemen—as well as Spain's king, Charles I.

The two Barbosas shared Magellan's and John's dream of sailing west to the Spice Islands. In October 1517, Magellan took the next necessary step. He left his once-beloved homeland and moved to Spain. Immediately, the explorer's luck improved. Diogo Barbosa arranged for Magellan to marry one of his daughters, Beatriz Barbosa, in December. All of a sudden, Magellan was a member of one of Spain's well-to-do families.

Diogo proceeded to show off his new son-in-law—and expert navigator—to members of Spain's high society. A well-known banker and spice trader, Cristóbal de Haro, formed an alliance with Magellan. So too did Ruy Faleiro, a Portuguese expatriate who specialized in mapmaking and astronomy.

A Meeting With the King

Eventually, Magellan's influential partners convinced Spanish officials to arrange a meeting between Magellan and King Charles. The king's power was seemingly unlimited. He not only ruled over the large country of Spain, but the New World (the Americas) was also under his control. Within a few years, he would inherit Germany, Austria, the Netherlands, and more.

Magellan had no idea how his meeting with the king would go. After all, Charles was just seventeen years old. He was new to the throne, ruling in place of his mentally ill mother, Joanna the Mad. Charles had been born in the Flemish city of Ghent, and he struggled to speak Spanish.

At their meeting, Magellan, his supporters, and the king spoke through interpreters. Much was discussed. Magellan assured Charles that although he was Portuguese, King Manuel had given him permission to serve another king. His friends hailed Magellan as the perfect man to lead the westward expedition to the Spice Islands. He had traveled to and lived in Asia, and he had

Jacques Reich did this etching of Charles V, Holy Roman Emperor from 1500 to 1558 (also known as Charles I of Spain) after the original portrait by Niccola Betonni.

displayed courage in battle. Moreover, he had fought to spread Christianity.

Magellan offered exciting news to the young ruler. He told him that, according to his calculations, the Spice Islands actually fell within Spain's domain. Faleiro, the astronomer, showed the king a chart that proved it. Magellan told King Charles that he could reach the Orient by sailing west through a strait in South America. He also showed Charles a globe that indicated that the ocean west of the Americas was not that large. It would be a fairly quick journey from South America to the Spice Islands.

That ocean, of course, is not nearly as small as Magellan thought it was. Nevertheless, he made his prospective quest sound believable to the teenage king. Magellan had won him over.

Anxious to launch the voyage, King Charles approved a written agreement on March 22, 1518. Magellan and Faleiro would serve as leaders of the westward voyage. They would command five ships, and each man would receive a generous salary of fifty thousand *maravedis* per year. They would be granted the title *adelantado* (governor) of all lands they discovered. If they discovered more than six islands, they could select up to two additional islands for themselves. In addition, Magellan and Faleiro were to receive a percentage of all net revenue (the total revenue minus the expenses) earned from their expedition. In a separate agreement, Magellan was given the power of life or death over all men on his fleet of ships.

As it turned out, Faleiro would not make the voyage. He suffered more and more from mental illness, and he eventually would become insane. Magellan alone would serve as the fleet's captain-general.

PLANNING THE VOYAGE

In a matter of months, Magellan had risen from a "nobody" to the leader of a highly anticipated expedition. After the agreement, he began to prepare for the journey. Preparations would take more than a year. Magellan first established a headquarters in Seville, along the Guadalquivir River. With money from the king and investors, he purchased five ships. The *San Antonio* (120 tons) was the largest and the *Santiago* the smallest. The *Trinidad*, *Concepción*, and *Victoria* were of sizes in between.

An experienced and well-trained seaman, Magellan oversaw the preparation of each ship. He also armed his ships as best as he could. He purchased dozens of mounted guns as well as body armor, small arms, and crossbows. He bought enough food to feed his crew for two years. He purchased literally hundreds of tons of biscuits, beans, cheese, onions, salted beef and pork, and more.

PEOPLE PROBLEMS

It was never easy for a commander to assemble a good crew, but Magellan faced exceptional difficulties. Although Magellan regarded the journey as a voyage of discovery, his influential friends viewed it as a moneymaking venture. Banker/trader Haro, for one, stocked the ships with goods that could be traded for spices.

In addition, top Spanish officials frustrated Magellan by installing their own officers and captains among the fleet. These men possessed inferior skills. Fortunately, Magellan enlisted enough talented Portuguese mariners to prevent disaster.

The crew problems seemed never ending. Many sailors, understandably, refused to go off on a voyage to the unknown. All the while, Portugal's King Manuel was trying to sabotage the venture. His spies infiltrated Seville and spread false rumors about Magellan.

The commander managed to assemble a crew of more than two hundred men. However, they came from many different countries—Spain, Portugal, Italy, England, Malaysia, and others— and spoke different languages. Spain and Portugal

Magellan's fleet of five ships—the *San Antonio, Santiago, Trinidad, Concepción,* and *Victoria*—set forth in 1519.

were longtime rivals, meaning conflict among sailors from those countries was likely.

Meanwhile, Magellan faced greater dangers from the ships' officers. He heard rumors that the Portuguese officers, working with King Manuel, would try to sabotage or obstruct the voyage.[3] Magellan also mistrusted the actions of Bishop

Fonseca. Although he was one of King Charles's chief counselors, Fonseca hated the fact that a Portuguese captain was commanding this important expedition rather than a Spaniard. The bishop used his influence to place his own Spanish agents in command of three of the five ships. Thus, Magellan could not trust any of his officers—Portuguese or Spanish.

FRUSTRATING DELAYS

Facing so many problems, Magellan was unable to launch his voyage in 1518, as King Charles had hoped. In fact, it was delayed by an entire year. On August 10, 1519, the five ships set sail on the Guadalquivir River. Yet, before Magellan's fleet reached the Atlantic Ocean, they discovered that many of the provisions had been stolen. The voyage was held up for nearly a month as more supplies were obtained.

Finally, on September 20, the crew prepared for departure. Magellan bid farewell to his wife, Beatriz, and infant son, Rodrigo. The sailors pulled up the anchors and raised the sails. And with that, the five Spanish ships ventured into the vast Atlantic Ocean.

Magellan had faced many threats and hardships in previous voyages. But nothing could prepare him for the dangers that lay ahead.

Chapter 5

THE SEARCH FOR EL PASO

Many fleets had departed for Asia over the years, but Magellan's ambitions were extraordinary. This expedition, wrote Magellan biographer Stefan Zweig, would be the "longest voyage of discovery, the boldest adventure in the records of our race."[1]

After departing on September 20, 1519, four ships followed the *Trinidad*, which was captained by Magellan. The first six days of their journey were uneventful, but that was about to change. On the twenty-sixth, the ships dropped anchor off the shore of Tenerife, a small island near the coast of West Africa. They went ashore for supplies and fresh water. But before they departed, a small boat from Spain arrived. A courier—sent by Magellan's father-in-law, Diogo Barbosa—delivered a secret letter to Ferdinand.[2]

Back in Spain, Barbosa wrote, friends of the three Spanish captains said that the trio was going to kill their Portuguese commander, Magellan. Those captains included Juan de Cartagena (on the *San Antonio*), Luis de Mendoza (*Victoria*), and Gaspar de Quesada (*Concepción*). Once

Magellan was dead, they would seize control of the fleet.

Magellan wrote back to Barbosa. He stated that since the captains had been appointed by the king, he would not take action against them. Instead, he would work with them and not give them any reason to revolt.

Tenerife is one of the Canary Islands near the coast of West Africa. This is where Magellan's ships first dropped anchor about six days into their journey.

Nevertheless, Magellan took the threat seriously—especially after meeting with all the captains before departing Tenerife. The Spaniards argued with Magellan throughout the meeting. Among other things, they insisted that they leave from Tenerife on a southwest course—not to the south as Magellan had planned. The captain-general agreed to their demands, not giving the captains any excuse to mutiny.

⬤ FEARS OF AN AMBUSH

On October 3, the five ships set sail, with the *Trinidad* in the lead. As promised, Magellan took a southwesterly course. But on the second day, he abruptly changed direction and sailed south. On the evening of the fifth, the *San Antonio* pulled up along the *Trinidad*. Captain Cartagena, undoubtedly angry, asked Magellan why he had broken his promise and changed direction. Magellan replied testily that

the other ships had only to follow his flag during the day and his farol (lamp) by night and should not ask questions.[3]

The southern course was indeed a slower route. However, Magellan feared that if he went southwest, he would have fallen into a trap. He sensed that Portugal's King Manuel had sent warships to that area to attack Magellan's ships. Had he sailed southwest, he might have been ambushed.

SHARKS, "FIRE," AND SOAKING RAIN

The fleet continued south, along the coast of Africa. Magellan may have avoided an ambush, but he faced further problems. First, his broken promise now gave the Spanish captains a reason to kill him. Worse yet, nature was turning against the fleet. Crew members noticed sharks swimming near the ships. In mid-October, a series of storms battered the ships so badly that the sailors almost had to cut away the masts.

During these storms, the sailors witnessed Saint Elmo's fire. These were ball-shaped electrostatic discharges that appeared at the mastheads. According to Italian sailor Antonio Pigafetta (whose journal would provide historians with valuable insights into the long voyage), the seamen interpreted the "fire" as a sign from the heavens. They wept at the sight. He wrote that for a few minutes, they were "blinded and calling for mercy, for truly we thought that we were dead men."[4]

Days after the storms, the seas became too calm. The fleet had entered the doldrums, an area of the ocean with very weak winds. Over twenty days, they sailed only nine miles. Moreover, rain soaked the sailors and the food, creating a bad rotting odor. Magellan had to cut food and water rations, and crew members grumbled. Cartagena blamed Magellan for leading them on this southerly course. For three days, he refused to let those on his ship salute Magellan.

CARTAGENA'S REBELLION

Eventually, the winds picked up, and in mid-November the sailors crossed the equator. A few days later, Magellan called all the captains to his flagship. They met for the court-martial of one of the crew members, who had acted inappropriately. However, as the five captains met in the *Trinidad*'s cabin, they began to argue about Magellan's leadership. The Spanish captains criticized Magellan, and Cartagena (the *San Antonio*'s captain) announced that he would no longer obey Magellan's commands.

Cartagena's pronouncement was an act of mutiny. As such, it gave Magellan reason to arrest

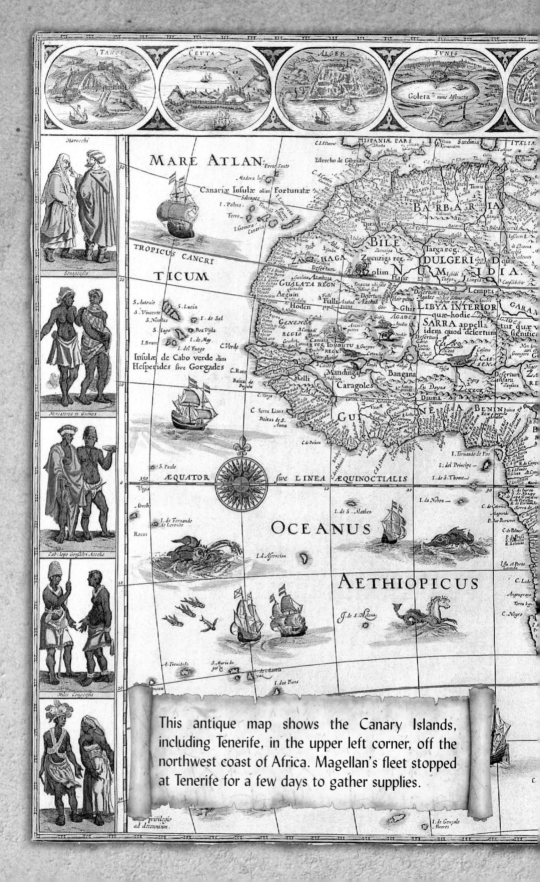

This antique map shows the Canary Islands, including Tenerife, in the upper left corner, off the northwest coast of Africa. Magellan's fleet stopped at Tenerife for a few days to gather supplies.

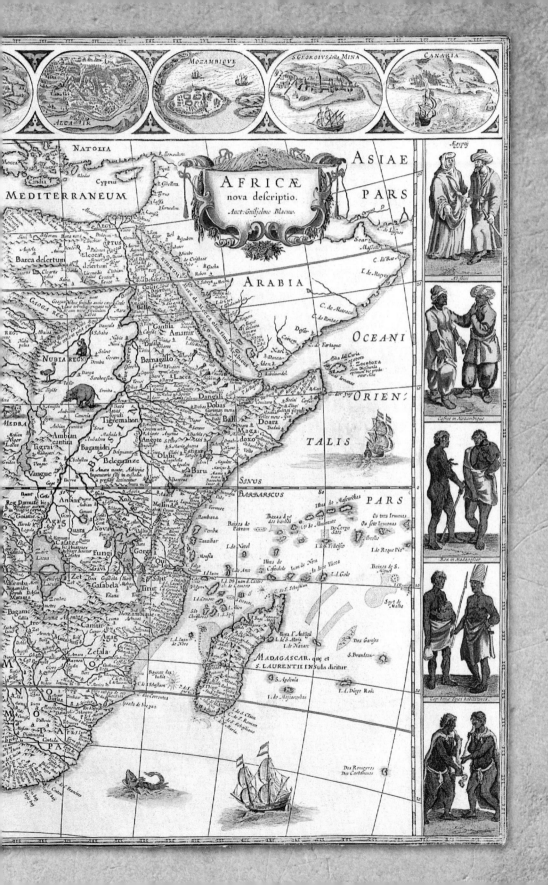

his number one enemy. He called in his armed guards to restrain Cartagena. The Spaniard pulled a knife, but he could offer no resistance. Cartagena was stripped of his captainship and imprisoned on the *Victoria*. Magellan named Antonio de Coca, a Spaniard and the fleet's accountant, as the *San Antonio*'s new captain.

REACHING SOUTH AMERICA

After crossing the equator, the ships traveled rapidly westward. On December 8, they saw land; they had made it to the coast of Brazil in South America. Crew members desperately needed to go ashore. They had been at sea for two months, and food and water were in short supply. Some were beginning to become ill from scurvy, a disease caused by lack of vitamin C.

But Magellan refused to go ashore and, instead, led the fleet southward down the Brazilian coast. He knew that they were still in Portuguese territory, and he feared that King Manuel's soldiers or navy might be waiting for them. In addition, reefs near the coast could destroy his ships if he tried to land there.

For five long days, they sailed south. Finally, after leaving Portuguese territory, they arrived at a spectacularly beautiful harbor: Rio de Janeiro. Today, the area is one of the most popular vacation spots in the world. At the time Magellan landed there, it was inhabited by naked natives. They proved to be friendly, which was lucky for the Portuguese: These natives were cannibals who customarily killed and ate the flesh of their enemies.

WILD TIMES IN RIO DE JANEIRO

As the seamen went ashore, they indulged in the land's abundant fruits and vegetables. Unbeknownst to these men, such foods contained the vitamin C they needed to prevent scurvy. Meanwhile, the natives eagerly traded animals for the Europeans' goods. As Pigafetta, the chronicler of this great expedition, wrote: "For one fishhook or one knife, those people gave five or six chickens; for one comb, a pair of geese; for one mirror or one pair of scissors, as many fish as would be sufficient for ten men."[5]

The crew spent two weeks on shore. The sailors socialized with the native women, while Magellan grumbled about his men's lack of discipline. Duarte Barbosa, Magellan's brother-in-law, went off for three days. The captain-general punished him by chaining him in irons.

Even more troublesome, Antonio de Coca (the *San Antonio*'s new captain) conspired with Luis de Mendoza (the *Victoria*'s captain) to release Cartagena. A furious Magellan arrested both Coca and

Magellan and his fleet stopped to rest at Rio de Janeiro. Here is a present-day picture of the city's harbor.

Cartagena. He named Álvaro de Mesquita the third and, he hoped, last captain of the *San Antonio*.

FALSE HOPE

After cleaning the ships and replenishing supplies, the mariners were ready to continue their journey. Departing around Christmas, their next goal was to find el paso, the anticipated passageway through the Americas. For more than two weeks, they sailed south down the coast. Finally, on January 11, 1520, they sighted three hills. Magellan's friend, John of Lisbon, had previously told Magellan that he believed this marked the opening of el paso.

Excited by the news, Magellan sent the *Santiago* to explore the waterway. The little ship was gone for two weeks, and when it returned the crew had bad news. The anticipated el paso was nothing more than a river that did not cross the continent. Not willing to abandon his dream, Magellan led his fleet to the supposed passage himself. Eventually, he drank the water. To his utter disappointment, it proved to be the fresh water of a river—not the salt water of an ocean.

At about this point in the expedition, Magellan began to show signs of obsession. Refusing to trust the *Santiago* crew was one thing. But now, even after his drink of fresh water, he persisted in further exploring the waterway. Magellan ordered his

men to man lifeboats. Together, they would keep exploring the river to find an outlet that led to a western ocean. It was hopeless. The men were stuck in what is now known as Río de la Plata. The river heads northwest and then due north.

The futile search lasted for nearly three weeks before Magellan finally called it off. John of Lisbon's prediction was wrong. So too was the map that Magellan had copied in King Manuel's treasury. The voyage itself, sponsored by King Charles, had been based on the assumption that el paso existed. Most of the crew members wanted to give up and go home, but Magellan insisted on continuing south. Somewhere, he believed (or hoped) that such a passageway had to exist.

FREEZING COLD

On February 2, the Spanish captains rounded up the crew and asked them what they wanted to do. Most voted to go back to Rio de Janeiro and stay through the Southern Hemisphere's winter. Since it was the middle of summer, they would stay there for many months. Magellan would not agree to this. He insisted that they continue southward in search of el paso. The next day, the fleet sailed again, despite the crew's protests.

Soon the crew believed that their leader had made a terrible mistake. The farther south they traveled, the colder it got. Winds blew ferociously,

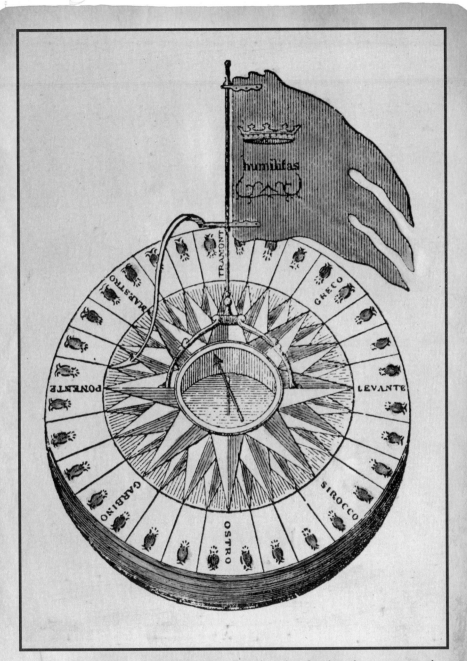

This illustration from Antonio Pigafetta's firsthand account of Magellan's circumnavigation of the world shows a sixteenth-century compass like the one Magellan would have used.

and storms left them soaked and chilled. The mast on the *Santiago* broke, and the *San Antonio* began to leak. The captains tried to stay close to shore in search of a strait to the western ocean, but this strategy added to the dangers. The *Victoria* became stuck on a sandbar before fortunately escaping.

For about two months, the sailors endured the cold and rough waters. Headwinds were so strong at times that they blew the ships backward. Magellan and the captains struggled just to keep the fleet together. Icebergs, which became more frequent as they sailed further south, were a potentially deadly hazard. Ice encrusted the ships' riggings and even clothing, and the crew was desperate for food. At one point, sailors landed on an islet to kill penguins and seals for meat.

Despite his determination to find el paso, Magellan realized that his crew was in grave danger. The sailors' hands and feet were frostbitten, and salt water on cracked skin caused painful sores. Finally, Magellan decided that the fleet would go ashore and winter in southern South America. In the country we know as Argentina, they found a cold, desolate location. Magellan named the area San Julián.

Seemingly no one cared for Magellan's plan— especially after he announced that food rations would have to be cut. After two frigid, horrific months at sea, the sailors would have to endure many more months of cold and hunger. Most crew members wanted to sail back north to find a warmer place to stay. In a meeting with Magellan, the fleet's captains argued emphatically to sail north. The captain-general refused.

◉ MUTINY

Sensing that a revolt was being planned, Magellan asked all the captains and pilots to eat with him on Sunday, April 1, after Mass. Only one of the men showed up. Throughout that day, a mutiny was in the works.

Not surprisingly, the Spanish captains led the revolt. Juan de Cartagena and Antonio de Coca, the former captains of the *San Antonio*, rowed to that ship that night. Gaspar de Quesada, captain of the *Concepción*, and thirty armed men joined them. After *San Antonio* sailors helped them onboard, the group seized the ship's current captain, Álvaro de Mesquita, and shackled him in chains. The small army then imprisoned most of the ship's crew.

The mutineers also controlled the *Victoria* and the *Concepció*n, giving them three of the five ships. The next morning, Magellan remained aboard the *Trinidad* while the enemy captains took the helm of the *San Antonio*. The Portuguese

captain-general may have been outnumbered, but he could outwit his Spanish rivals.

On the *Trinidad* and *Santiago*, Magellan ordered his men to arms. Later in the day, he saw a lifeboat filled with sailors rowing from the *San Antonio* to the *Concepción*. They could not handle the strong current, however, and wound up tossed toward the *Trinidad*. With the men pleading for help, Magellan's crew assisted them aboard. The captain-general befriended the sailors, offering them drinks of wine. In return, the men told him the details of the captains' rebellion.

MAGELLAN'S INGENIOUS PLAN

Armed with this information, Magellan came up with a brilliant plan. First, he ordered his *Trinidad* sailors to change clothes with the rescued men from the *San Antonio*. Next, his loyal sailors (in their imposter clothes) rowed past the rival *Victoria*. He also sent another boat toward the *Victoria*. One of the men announced that he had a letter for Captain Mendoza. Since the sailors in the boat seemed unarmed, the mutineers allowed them on the *Victoria*.

The man did not have a message for Mendoza but rather a dagger, with which he stabbed the captain to death. Swiftly, the imposter sailors boarded the *Victoria* and took control of it. Three of the ships were now under Magellan's control, and he had another plan in mind. Per his orders, his trio of ships crept slowly toward the harbor. They blocked the harbor's entrance, leaving the *Concepción* and *San Antonio* vulnerable in the water.

Quesada tried to lead the *San Antonio* through the blockade. He was not only unsuccessful, but Magellan loyalists boarded the *San Antonio* and captured him. Now outnumbered four ships to one, Cartagena surrendered. Those who had questioned Magellan's competence now marveled at how he had prevented the attempted coup.

SENTENCING

For five days, the rebels were put on trial. Forty men were sentenced to death, but this was only a formality. Showing great leniency, Magellan sentenced the mutineers to hard labor: cleaning and repair work while shackled in chains. Several months later, he would pardon them all.

Only Quesada, who had mortally stabbed an officer, was executed (by beheading). Cartagena, Magellan's chief nemesis, was simply confined to a cabin. Magellan knew it would be unwise to execute him because of his influential connections back in Spain. However, when Cartagena and a priest were later caught plotting another rebellion, Magellan marooned them on shore.

THOSE WITH BIG FEET

Though the mutiny attempt was over, the crew faced a brutal winter. It was already bitterly cold, and the temperatures would drop even lower from April through August. Meanwhile, the food supply was low. Magellan directed some of his men to fish and hunt.

In San Julián, Magellan's crew saw animals they were unfamiliar with, including llamas and penguins. After two months, they saw a native for the first time. Pigafetta, for one, was astonished. The man was naked with red and yellow paint on his face. His hair was painted white. He danced and sang and threw dust on his head. More shockingly, the man was huge. "He was so tall that we reached only to his waist, and he was well proportioned," Pigafetta wrote.[6]

Later, the crew saw other natives. The men were extremely tall. Had their waistlines truly been as high as the Europeans' heads, they would have stood at least nine feet tall. Magellan named the people Patagonians, meaning those with big feet. At first, the crew and the natives got along well. Magellan gave one of the men clothes and other items. "He left us very joyous and happy," Pigafetta wrote. "The following day, he brought one of those large animals to the captain-general."[7]

Magellan and his crew had never seen penguins before.

The Europeans and Patagonians might have gotten along peacefully through the winter. However, when the crew tried to capture two of the Patagonians to take with them, the natives turned hostile. During the struggle, one of the crew members was killed.

The Europeans never captured one of the "giants," although later explorers to the region would also report their presence. In a 1773 book published in England, explorers James Cook and John Byron reported that the men were roughly six feet, six inches tall—not nine feet. Mysteriously, over time, this group of people seemed to disappear. Today, the natives of the region are actually shorter than average.

In all, the fleet spent five months at San Julián. During that time, the sailors careened the ships: they scraped the ships' bottoms, caulked seams, and secured braces. Meanwhile, Magellan sent Captain Juan Rodríguez Serrano and the *Santiago* on a southerly trip to find el paso. After two weeks, Serrano found not a passage but a bay, which he named Santa Cruz.

THE WRECK OF THE SANTIAGO

Upon his return to San Julián, Serrano faced ferocious winds. He temporarily landed the *Santiago* on a sandbank, but the relentless weather sunk the ship. Most of Juan Serrano's thirty-seven-man crew made it to shore, but one man died and the ship's cargo was lost.

The men may have been left for dead were it not for two brave sailors. The duo traveled by foot to San Julián, finally arriving after eleven days. Magellan personally sailed to rescue the stranded mariners. Upon witnessing the Santa Cruz harbor, he decided that the crew would winter there

In 1520, Magellan and his crew spent time in Patagonia (near Argentina), where they encountered the tall (more than six feet) people who lived there.

instead. They took with them a Patagonian "giant" whom they named Juan Gigante.

The crew spent the next couple months fishing, hunting, and trapping. Not only did they need to feed themselves each day, but Magellan wanted to get more food for their spring journey. He still believed that el paso existed. Once they found it and passed through it, the four remaining ships would sail across the unknown waters to the Spice Islands.

A large number of sailors wanted to return to Europe, but Magellan convinced the fleet to follow his command. By October, they were ready to set sail. Only four ships remained. Magellan captained the flagship, the *Trinidad*, while Álvaro de Mesquita commanded the *San Antonio*. Juan Serrano and Duarte Barbosa captained the *Concepción* and *Victoria*, respectively. They left Santa Cruz for good on October 18, 1520.

POSSIBLY EL PASO?

It was not long before the fleet faced another perilous situation. A powerful storm, with winds roaring up from Antarctica, pounded the ships. Despite the weather, the fleet sailed southward and discovered a bay. Magellan ordered the captains of the *San Antonio* and *Concepción* to explore the inlet for a possible passageway through the continent. As days passed, the *Trinidad* and

Victoria bobbed in the water during another merciless storm.

The bad weather eventually passed, but the *San Antonio* and *Concepción* did not return. Magellan became worried. He saw smoke in the bay area and wondered if it was a signal of distress. However, after four days away, the *San Antonio* and *Concepción* finally returned. Moreover, the crews on both ships were jubilant. They cheered, flew pennants, and fired salutes. They believed, after so many months, that they had found the exclusive el paso.

The two ships had sailed through the bay to a narrow waterway, which they entered. That led to a large bay and then another narrow channel. They drank the water, which tasted like salt. Undoubtedly, the unknown ocean lay ahead.

Excited and inspired, Magellan led his fleet into the bay. Soon they spotted a man-made structure on shore. Hoping it was a village, Magellan sent ten men to explore. They found only a native burial ground—plus bleached bones and a rotting whale carcass on the beach. Spooked by it all, the sailors returned to the ships. Magellan pressed forward.

On October 27, the ships anchored at Paso Real. Magellan called for a meeting with his captains and pilots, asking them if they should attempt the voyage across the unchartered ocean.

One of the men objected, but the others were willing to take the risk. So too, of course, was Magellan. "[E]ven though we may be forced to eat the leather chafing gear on the yards," he told them, "we must go forward and discover what has been promised to the Emperor." He added, "God will help us and bring us good fortune."[8]

THROUGH THE NARROW STRAIT

Thus began the journey to the unknown. The voyage through el paso, which Magellan called the Strait of All Saints, proved treacherous. It was narrow and mazelike with many obstacles, such as numerous little islands. On October 31, Gonzalo Gómez de Espinosa and others paddled ahead on a lifeboat to explore the strait. Also, Magellan sent the San Antonio on an exploratory mission as well. Meanwhile, the crew hunted and fished, hoping to store up enough food for their long journey ahead.

After several days, Gómez and his small crew returned, claiming they had found the route to the ocean. Wrote Pigafetta, "The captain-general wept for joy, and called that cape 'Cape Deseado,' for we had been desiring it for a long time."[9]

The San Antonio, however, did not come back. Days passed, and Magellan became concerned. His search parties proved fruitless. Unbeknownst to the captain-general, San Antonio pilot Estevão

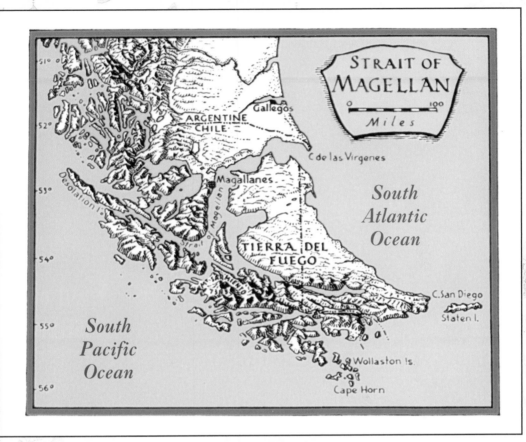

By the end of 1520, Magellan's fleet had discovered "the Strait of All Saints," a treacherous passageway at the southern tip of South America. The strait—known today as the Strait of Magellan—would lead them to the Pacific Ocean.

Gomes—who despised Magellan—had taken over the ship. Gomes clapped Captain Mesquita in chains and sailed back to Spain.

Magellan was now down to three ships. Worse, because the *San Antonio* was the largest of the ships, it had carried a great deal of provisions. The fleet's food supplies were now dangerously low.

STRAIT OF
MAGELLAN

This NASA satellite photo shows the Strait of Magellan.

Again, the captain-general asked his officers if they thought they should continue. As loyalists of Magellan, they stated that they should. On November 26, the three ships pulled up anchor at Río del Isleo and forged ahead.

Before reaching the ocean, the fleet sailed through the last stretch of the Strait of All Saints, which would eventually be renamed the Strait of Magellan. On November 28, Pigafetta wrote that "we debouched from that strait, engulfing ourselves in the Pacific Sea."[10]

To a man, the crew members knew that a long and perhaps agonizing journey lay ahead. What they didn't realize was that the ocean was much larger—actually, several times bigger—than virtually everyone expected.

Chapter 6

Across the Great Pacific

For centuries, the journey of Christopher Columbus has been hailed as the greatest of the Age of Discovery. But, argues Magellan biographer Stefan Zweig, "even that journey is not to be deemed comparable with the one made by Magellan amid unspeakable hardships and privations."[1]

Columbus's journey to the Americas, with well-stocked ships, lasted thirty-three days. When Magellan's fleet reached the far side of el paso in late November 1520, they had been away for fifteen months—and most of their journey still lay ahead.

Unlike Columbus's ships, the *Trinidad*, *Victoria*, and *Concepción* lacked adequate food. The sailors were feeling the effects of extreme weather and poor diets. Their clothing was torn and tattered. The ships' rigging and sails had taken a beating. In this ragged condition, the fleet prepared to traverse the unfamiliar waters before them. Magellan named the ocean Mar Pacifico (Pacific Ocean), which is Spanish for "calm sea."

The first three weeks of the Pacific Ocean journey went well. Magellan headed due north, staying in sight of the

South American coast. Strong winds pushed them along at a rapid rate. After months of frigid temperatures, the weather turned much warmer. The sailors kept from starving by catching and eating fish. "But even with this modest addition to their food supplies," wrote a Magellan biographer, Hawthorne Daniel, "and despite a rigid reduction in their rations, their already inadequate provisions decreased alarmingly."[2]

In mid-December, Magellan changed course, heading northwest. According to his maps, Asia was not that far away. Magellan had relied heavily on the estimates of Ruy Faleiro. This Portuguese astronomer had calculated that the ocean was not exceptionally wide. He was wrong. The Pacific is the largest ocean in the world.

Day after day, sailors searched in vain for land. At night, they stared at the stars. Pigafetta and others noticed that the stars viewed from the Southern Hemisphere were much different from those in the Northern Hemisphere. "Many small stars clustered together are seen," Pigafetta wrote, "which have the appearance of two clouds of mist with little distance between them, and they are somewhat dim."[3] These "clustered stars" are actually galaxies, and they are only visible in the Southern Hemisphere. Astronomers today call them "Magellanic Clouds."

PUTRID WATER, ROTTEN FOOD

Weeks passed, with still no land in sight. By late December and into January 1521, sailors must have surely sensed that death was at hand. The winds became calmer, and progress was slow. They fished day after day, but their catches were alarmingly infrequent. Rain did not fall and, unknown to anyone, some of the water casks (containers) had begun to leak. The water in other

Astronomers named galaxies seen only in the Southern Hemisphere "Magellanic clouds" because Magellan and his men were the first Europeans to view these clusters of stars.

casks turned bad, and the sailors were forced to drink yellow putrid water.

The condition of the remaining food was at least as bad. "[W]e ate biscuit," Pigafetta wrote, "which was no longer biscuit, but powder of biscuits swarming with worms, for they had eaten the good." In addition, he wrote that "it stank strongly of the urine of rats."[4]

More and more, the sailors became ill. The hot sun, the weeks at sea, the lack of nutrition, plus the wretched food and water left them listless and diseased. By the middle of January, some of the men had died. Dozens were unable to walk.

The crew spotted an island on January 24, but tragically it was all rock. San Pablo, as it was named, was formed from the walls of a volcano; its crater lay underwater. Nevertheless, a great deal of fish and seafood proliferated near the island. The sailors ate until they were full, and they brought more food onboard. When a storm broke out, they collected rainwater on their sails and stored it for later. Unfortunately, they found no fruits or vegetables. The men again were suffering from scurvy.

THE DEATH TOLL MOUNTS

The fleet continued on, but conditions got worse. They sailed northwest, getting even closer to the equator. As the days passed, they ran out of real food. They caught and ate rats. They scraped sawdust off food barrels, wet it down into a paste, and swallowed it. They even tried to eat soaked leather. Scurvy took a horrible toll. The men's gums swelled, making eating extremely difficult. According to Pigafetta, nineteen crew members—plus the Patagonian and a native of Brazil—died from the disease.

The ships sailed at a good pace due to strong winds, but Magellan did not know what lay ahead. Late in February, the captain-general changed course from northwest to due west. Had he not done so, ironically enough, he would have spotted the Hawaiian Islands. He would have been the first European to reach that bountiful paradise.

Though he was more than forty years old, Magellan displayed almost superhuman stamina. He cared for the sick after the ship's doctor died, and took over the sailors' duties after they were too weak and ill to do so. Eventually, the mariners lacked the strength to lower the sails in the evening. Thus, they sailed straight through the nights. Though night travel allowed them to move forward, they risked crashing into rocks or coral reefs. Such a collision could sink a ship.

Like those stranded in the desert, the delirious sailors sometimes saw illusions. "Land ho!" one would cry, but only water lay ahead. On March 6, however, a lookout truly did spot land—not just

one island, but three. They sailed closer to one of the islands during the night, and in the morning they saw canoes and huts on the shore. The fleet had reached the island of Guam.

THE RAID OF GUAM

Since the sailors were too weak to lower the sails, Magellan ordered that the ropes holding them be cut. They also dropped anchor. In their feeble

state, the last thing the sailors needed was hostile natives. Yet there they came, paddling to the ships in painted boats with sails made of palm leaves. The naked invaders boarded the ships with clubs and spears and stole whatever they could carry. The natives overpowered most of the sailors, but some of the Europeans fought back with bows and arrows.

Later, Magellan responded with vengeance. He mustered a crew of forty armed men and stormed the island. The small army killed some men and burned many boats and at least forty houses. Frightened, the natives retreated farther back on the island. Returning the next day, Magellan's men obtained what they desperately needed. Through a combination of force and bartering, they gathered fresh water, fish, bananas, coconuts, sweet potatoes, and sugarcane—as well as a pig.

Magellan's fleet reached the island of Guam in March 1521. This modern-day photo shows the coast of Guam.

On March 9, Magellan was ready to set sail again. He feared another attack from those on the islands, which the crew dubbed *Islas de los Ladrones* (Thieves' Islands). He also believed that they were reaching the western part of the ocean. The Orient must be near. Again, it was another life-risking gamble by the captain-general. His crew had enough food to last only a few days.

Proof That the World Is Round

This time, Magellan's instincts proved correct. After traveling more than a thousand miles in seven days, they saw islands ahead. On March 18, a boat carrying a small group of islanders journeyed to the ships. After the islanders returned to shore, Pigafetta wrote that "their chief went immediately to the captain-general, giving signs of joy because of our arrival."[5] Friendly natives climbed aboard the *Trinidad,* trading food for such goods as bells and mirrors.

On March 25, the fleet sailed on, taking a southwesterly route. Three days later, they came upon another island. Islanders in a canoe rowed out to greet them. Magellan's slave, Enrique de Malacca, spoke to the islanders in Malayan. Remarkably, they responded in the same language.

Magellan had captured Enrique back in 1509 while in the Malayan Peninsula in Southeast Asia.

Now, it appeared, they had reached that general area. Specifically, the fleet had reached an archipelago (a group or chain of islands) known as the Philippines, which was part of the greater Malay Archipelago.

The implications were profound. It meant that Magellan and his fleet were the first-known people to traverse the Pacific Ocean, a voyage that had taken 110 days. They also had traveled more

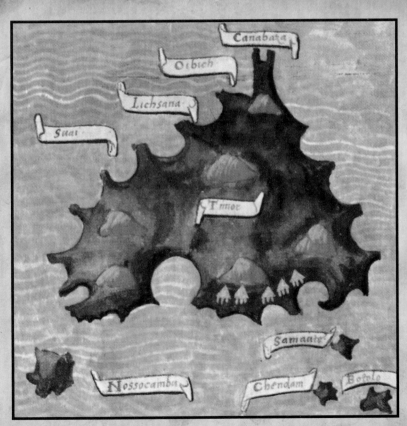

Antonio Pigafetta drew this map of Timor, an island in the Malay Archipelago, in 1521.

than halfway around the world, another first. Magellan achieved his and his king's objective—to reach the Orient, today known as Asia, by sailing west. By doing so, he proved beyond a doubt that the world was round. With the records of Magellan's journey, mapmakers could better estimate the width of the Pacific and the size of planet Earth. Indeed, March 28, 1521, was one of the most momentous days in the history of exploration.

A Pleasant Stay on Limasawa

Though the islanders shared a language with Enrique the slave, they did not trust the European visitors. They paddled back to shore. About two hours later, two large boats traveled to the ships. One carried Rajah Kolambu, the ruler of the Philippine island of Limasawa. Kolambu talked to Enrique but did not board the ship, although some of his people did. Magellan greeted them with kindness, and they responded by offering gold and ginger on behalf of the rajah. The captain-general displayed his gratitude but did not accept the gift.

As we have seen, relations between the Europeans and island natives were often hostile during the Age of Discovery. Such was not the case with Magellan and Kolambu. With Enrique as interpreter, they talked the next day. They even tasted each other's blood as a sign of strong friendship.

For the first time in the expedition, Magellan did not seem anxious to move on. Some of his crew wanted to sail to the Spice Islands, which was the fleet's ultimate objective. But Magellan wanted to explore the Philippines a little more. His fleet stayed on Limasawa for a full week.

In general, the two groups got along well. The Europeans celebrated Good Friday and Easter Mass, which the islanders attended. The sailors helped harvest the rice crop and enjoyed the natives' harvest festival. The men engaged in trading, with the Europeans getting the best of their iron-for-gold transactions.

THE CHRISTIANIZING OF CEBU

In early April, the fleet sailed for the island of Cebu. This island was larger than Limasawa, and its people—Kolambu told Magellan—were wealthier. Kolambu and some of his people accompanied the Spanish fleet to Cebu. As they approached the shore, they saw large houses built along the shore as well as hundreds of canoes.

Upon arrival, Magellan's ships fired a loud salute. Though it was meant to be a friendly greeting, the king of Cebu, Humabon, was unsure what to make of Magellan's arrival. Humabon conferred with a merchant from Siam, who said that these were men who had conquered India, Calicut, and Malacca. Not wanting to endure their wrath, Humabon welcomed the visitors.

King Humabon allowed his people to trade with the Europeans. On April 14, Humabon and his wife were baptized as Christians. So too, in a grand and solemn ceremony, were five hundred of

Magellan planted a cross upon his arrival in Cebu City in April 1521. It is believed that the cross above, in a small chapel in the city, is a replica of the original cross.

their subjects. Zealous about his faith, Magellan certainly took pride in the baptism of so many. Wrote Pigafetta: "The captain told the king through the interpreter that he thanked God for inspiring the king to become a Christian."[6] The conversions did not end. Over a two-week period, Magellan's priests baptized thousands of natives from Cebu and neighboring islands.

However, not everyone was willing to convert to Christianity. Lapulapu, a chieftain of nearby Mactan Island, was one such holdout. The chieftain, in fact, disdained Christianity and refused to swear allegiance to the Spanish king. Humabon hated Lapulapu, who had long fought with him over control of land. Humabon sensed that Magellan, who was fiercely loyal to his lord and his king, would become angry at the news of Lapulapu's obstinance. His instinct was correct, and Humabon suggested that he and Magellan lead an army to Mactan and kill Lapulapu.

MAGELLAN'S DEMISE

Throughout the long expedition, Magellan believed that God would protect him. His faith must have played a role in his planned invasion of Mactan, for he certainly did not have the manpower to defeat the enemy.

Most of Magellan's fleet, most notably his Spanish captains, would not fight. Magellan mustered an army of only sixty men. Forty-eight of them would be armored, with swords, shields, axes, guns, and crossbows. During the wee hours of April 27, they sailed to Mactan. Humabon and hundreds of Cebuans went with them. However, upon reaching Mactan that morning, Magellan declared that only his European men would fight.

Because of the rocks and corals near the shore, Magellan's forces could not land on Mactan. Instead, forty-nine of them leaped into thigh-high water and walked to shore. When they reached land, according to Pigagetta, more than fifteen hundred warriors awaited them. "When they saw us," he wrote, "they charged down upon us with exceeding loud cries."[7]

The invaders were outmanned thirty to one. Magellan ordered the burning of houses, hoping that would scare off the enemy. But it simply roused them to greater fury. One of them shot Magellan in his right leg with a poisoned arrow. Realizing that the situation was hopeless, the captain-general ordered his men to retreat. All did except for a half dozen or so who remained with Magellan.

According to Pigafetta, the natives focused their attention on the leader, Magellan. They struck his arm with a bamboo spear and slashed one of his legs with a sword. While under assault,

Pigafetta wrote, Magellan managed to kill one of the islanders with his lance. But the natives overwhelmed Magellan, stabbing and slashing him to death with spears and swords. Pigafetta, who was wounded, and the other Europeans were able to escape.

In retrospect, Magellan's invasion of Mactan seems utterly senseless—his death a waste. Yet Magellan had always been a man of grand ambitions. He had attempted and achieved

The Mactan people killed Magellan during a battle in 1521.

unprecedented feats on the high seas. He had spread Christianity to thousands on the islands. Thus, it made sense that Magellan pushed himself to the limits, to the point of death. His loyal sailors lamented the loss of their loyal and courageous leader. Wrote Pigafetta: "[T]hey killed our mirror, our light, our comfort, and our true guide."[8]

TWENTY-SEVEN SLAIN

After the defeat at Mactan, the Europeans were extra anxious to set sail. Juan Serrano, a Magellan loyalist, was chosen as one of the new leaders of the fleet. But before they departed, Humabon plotted to slaughter his European guests. Magellan biographer Tim Joyner explains:

> [H]e realized that the defeat by Lapulapu and outrage at the behavior of the ship's crews toward the island's women was causing his subjects to question his leadership. . . . There can be little doubt that Lapulapu also urged Humabon to get rid of his troublesome guests. Already disgusted with them, Humabon resolved to do just that.[9]

Humabon hatched a sinister scheme. He invited the fleet's high-ranking crew members to a feast on May 1. At that time, they would be presented with jewels for the king of Spain. Twenty-seven members of the fleet attended the feast. Each one, including Serrano and Duarte Barbosa (Magellan's brother-in-law), was slain.

SAILING ON

The fleet left Cebu as soon as possible, with João Lopes Carvalho the new captain-general. Of the 241 members of the original crew, only 115 remained. Because they did not have enough men to maintain three ships, they burned the *Concepción*. Now only the *Trinidad* and *Victoria* remained.

Carvalho's fleet sailed west past the many islands of Southeast Asia. They stopped at Borneo, the third largest island in the world. Relations with Borneo's people were friendly at first, but trouble ensued and some of the sailors were detained. The fleet moved on, but—without Magellan to lead them—discipline disintegrated. After careening at an island near Borneo in August, Carvalho was ousted as commander. The crew elected Gonzalo Gómez de Espinosa as their new leader and captain of the *Trinidad,* and Juan Sebastian Elcano took command of the *Victoria*.

For weeks, the two ships continued west. Finally, on November 8, 1521, they reached their original goal: the Spice Islands. Magellan had told King Charles that his fleet would reach these islands by sailing west, and now the promise had been fulfilled. Unfortunately, the western route had proven to be an utterly impractical way to

reach the Spice Islands. It had taken the fleet nearly two years and three months to reach them, at the cost of most of its crew.

BACK TO SPAIN

As it turned out, only the *Victoria* made the journey from the Spice Islands back to Spain. The *Trinidad* leaked badly and could not make the trip. Needing repairs, the ship remained at Tidore; much of the crew stayed behind as well. After making repairs, the *Trinidad* was to sail toward Panama. However, the Portuguese captured the ship.[10]

Elcano, one of the mutiny leaders back in San Julián, struggled to captain the *Victoria* home. His ship included a small crew, many of whom were ill. While crossing ten thousand miles of ocean, they constantly had to pump out water from the chronically leaking ship. They wanted to stop at the Azores Islands for repairs, but feared attacks by the Portuguese. Nonetheless, the ship needed supplies badly and did make a brief stop at the Portuguese-held Cape Verde Islands.

Finally, in early September 1522, the *Victoria* arrived at Seville, Spain, with a crew of twenty-one men (among them three Moluccan natives). It had taken them three years and four weeks, but these sailors had achieved an extraordinary feat.

They were the first people in history to sail around the world. These are the men who achieved immortality:

Juan Sebastian Elcano, captain-general

Miguel de Rodas, boatswain (contramaestre) of the *Victoria*

Francisco Albo, of Axio, boatswain of the *Trinidad*

Juan de Acurio, of Bermeo, boatswain of the *Concepción*

Maartin de Judicibus, of Genoa, superintendent of the *Concepción*

Hernando de Bustamante, of Alcantara, barber of the *Concepción*

Juan de Zuvileta, of Baracaldo, page of the *Victoria*

Miguel Sanchez, of Rodas, skilled seaman (marinero) of the *Victoria*

Nicholas the Greek, of Naples, marinero of the *Victoria*

Diego Gallego, of Bayonne, marinero of the *Victoria*

Juan Rodriguez, of Seville, marinero of the *Trinidad*

Antonio Rodriguez, of Huelva, marinero of the *Trinidad*

Francisco Rodriguez, of Seville (a Portuguese), marinero of the *Concepción*

Juan de Arratia, of Bilbao, common sailor (grumete) of the *Victoria*

Vasco Gomez Gallego (a Portuguese), grumete of the *Trinidad*

Juan de Santandres, of Cueto, grumete of the *Trinidad*

Martin de Isaurraga, of Bermeo, grumete of the *Concepción*

The Chevalier Antonio Pigafetta, of Vicenza, passenger[11]

These heroic mariners were greeted by naval cannons and cheering crowds. Barefoot and dressed in rags, the sailors walked to Our Lady of Victory, a church once frequented by Ferdinand Magellan. There, they prayed and gave thanks for returning safely.

The former King Charles, who by 1522 was known as Emperor Charles V of the Holy Roman Empire, displayed gratitude to the fleet that had set out under Magellan. They had not found a short route to the West, and the spices they brought back barely covered the cost of the expedition. However, they had brought honor to Spain by circumnavigating the globe. Charles rewarded Elcano with a generous annual pension as well as a special coat of arms. It bore a globe that came with the motto *Primus circumdedisti me* ("First to go around me").

The *Victoria* was the only ship in Magellan's fleet to survive the trip around the world.

ONE DAY OFF

When the *Victoria* returned to Spain, its crew was convinced that it was September 7. They had been meticulous in their date logging, checking off a day for every time the sun rose. The people of Seville, however, insisted that it was September 8. Certainly, a whole city could not be wrong about the date.

It turned out that the fleet had kept perfect records. But by traveling westward around the globe, they saw one less sunrise than if they had remained in place. News of this phenomenon caused quite a stir, and a delegation was created to explain it to the pope.

This discovery made people realize the need for an international dateline. Eventually, that imaginary line would be established in the Pacific Ocean. Those who cross the line while traveling west must add twenty-four hours (and vice versa for traveling east). Had Magellan's fleet added that extra day, their recorded date would have matched the one in Seville: September 8, 1522.

MAGELLAN: THE DRIVING FORCE

Without Magellan's perseverance and leadership, the fleet never would have achieved its epic feat. He was the man who led the reluctant crew through South America's *el paso*—now known as the Strait of Magellan. He was the leader who achieved the herculean feat of traversing the Pacific Ocean.

Only tragedy would have awaited Magellan's arrival. When he had departed Spain in 1519, he left behind an infant son, Rodrigo. In addition, his wife, Beatriz, had been pregnant at the time. But while Magellan was away, Rodrigo had died and his second child was dead at birth. Beatriz died in

The ship-shaped "Monument to the Discoveries" in Lisbon, Portugal, was built in 1960 to honor the five hundredth anniversary of the death of Prince Henry the Navigator (left). Also pictured are Magellan (sixth from left) and Vasco da Gama (third from left).

her father's house in March 1522, six months before the *Victoria* returned. Moreover, Elcano—a Spaniard—frequently defamed the Portuguese-born Magellan.

Though many of the crew perished, we are fortunate that Antonio Pigafetta was among the survivors. His chronicle provides us with many of the details of their epic expedition. Throughout his diary, Pigafetta consistently lauded his captain-general. Magellan's strength of character may have been his greatest trait. "Among the other virtues which he possessed," Pigafetta wrote, "he was more constant than anyone else in the greatest of adversity."[12]

Chapter Notes

Chapter 1. The Humiliation
1. Tim Joyner, *Magellan* (Camden, Maine: International Marine Publishing, 1992), p. 34.

Chapter 2. The Quest for Cheaper Pepper
1. Stefan Zweig, *Conqueror of the Seas: The Story of Magellan* (New York: Blue Ribbon Books, 1940), p. 3.

Chapter 3. Growing Up in the Royal Court
1. Henry Harrisse, *The Diplomatic History of America: Its First Chapter* (London: Stevens, 1897), p. ii (map of Treaty of Tordesillas).

Chapter 4. Gentleman Adventurer
1. Tim Joyner, *Magellan* (Camden, Maine: International Marine Publishing, 1992), p. 48.
2. Stefan Zweig, *Conqueror of the Seas: The Story of Magellan* (New York: Blue Ribbon Books, 1940), p. 53.
3. Joyner, p. 95.

Chapter 5. The Search for El Paso
1. Stefan Zweig, *Conqueror of the Seas: The Story of Magellan* (New York: Blue Ribbon Books, 1940), p. 144.
2. Tim Joyner, *Magellan* (Camden, Maine: International Marine Publishing, 1992), p. 120.
3. Ibid., p. 121.
4. Antonio Pigafetta, *The First Voyage Around the World,* ed. Theodore J. Cuchey Jr. (New York: Marsilio Publishers, 1995), p. 8.
5. Ibid., p. 9.
6. Ibid., p. 14.
7. Ibid., p. 16.
8. Tim Joyner, *Magellan* (Camden, Maine: International Marine Publishing, 1992), p. 154.

9. Pigafetta, p. 23.

10. Ibid., p. 26.

Chapter 6. Across the Great Pacific

1. Stefan Zweig, *Conqueror of the Seas: The Story of Magellan* (New York: Blue Ribbon Books, 1940), p. 223.

2. Hawthorne Daniel, *Ferdinand Magellan* (Garden City, N.Y.: Doubleday & Company, Inc., 1964), p. 226.

3. Antonio Pigafetta, *The First Voyage Around the World,* ed. Theodore J. Cuchey Jr. (New York: Marsilio Publishers, 1995), p. 27.

4. Ibid., p. 26.

5. Ibid., p. 31.

6. Ibid., p. 51.

7. Ibid., p. 60.

8. Ibid., p. 61.

9. Tim Joyner, *Magellan* (Camden, Maine: International Marine Publishing, 1992), p. 196.

10. Daniel, p. 273.

11. The Mariners' Museum, "Ferdinand Magellan: And Then There Was One," n.d., <http://www.mariner.org/exploration/index.php?type=explorersection&id=10> (January 27, 2007).

12. Daniel, p. 276.

Glossary

ambush—An attack by those who are in hiding.

aristocrat—A member of the nobility or the privileged class.

astronomer—A scientist who studies the stars and planets.

caravel—A small, fast, and easily maneuverable ship used by the Portuguese and Spanish beginning in the 1400s.

careen—To turn a ship on its side in shallow water and clean and repair the ship's exterior bottom.

carrack—A sailing ship of the fifteenth and sixteenth centuries.

cask—A barrel that holds liquids.

channel—A deep and narrow waterway through which ships pass.

circumnavigate—To travel completely around the world.

coup—The sudden overthrow of those in charge.

crossbow—A weapon that fires arrows.

crosswinds—Winds that blow against the side of a ship or boat.

equator—The imaginary line that separates the Northern Hemisphere and the Southern Hemisphere.

expedition—A journey, often sponsored by a government, organized for a particular purpose.

flagship—The ship within a fleet that carries the commander.

fleet—A group of ships on the same mission.

harbor—A body of water adjacent to shore where boats and ships can dock while they are loaded or unloaded.

headwinds—Winds that blow directly against the course of a ship.

holy crusade—A war waged on behalf of the attackers' religion.

jousting—A competition in which a knight on horseback tries to knock the opposing knight off his horse.

mariner—A person who works on a ship.

maritime—Relating to the sea or sailing.

marooned—To be stranded on an island.

merchant—A person who sells goods.

mutiny—A rebellion against the ship's (or ships') leader (or leaders).

navigation—The science of directing or plotting the course of a vessel.

page—A young male servant.

quartermaster—A military officer who is in charge of supplies.

ration—A restricted amount of food and other consumables.

reef—A ridge of rock or coral just below the water's surface.

royal court—The household of the king or queen.

sabotage—A deliberate act of destruction designed to hinder the nemesis's plans.

salute—A firing of weapons on a ship; meant to serve as a greeting.

scurvy—A disease caused by a deficiency of vitamin C.

squire—A young knight in training.

strait—A narrow area of water that connects two larger bodies of water.

viceroy—A governor of a country or province who represents his or her king or queen.

Further Reading

Books

Bailey, Katharine. *Ferdinand Magellan: Circumnavigating the World.* New York: Crabtree, 2005.

Bergreen, Laurence. *Over the Edge of the World: Magellan's Terrifying Circumnavigation of the Globe.* New York: Harper Perennial, 2004.

Hoogenboom, Lynn. *Ferdinand Magellan: A Primary Source Biography.* New York: Rosen, 2006.

Kramer, Sydelle. *Who Was Ferdinand Magellan?* New York: Grosset & Dunlap, 2004.

Petrie, Kristin. *Ferdinand Magellan.* Edina, Minn.: ABDO, 2007.

Whiting, Jim. *Ferdinand Magellan.* Hockessin, Del.: Mitchell Lane, 2006.

Zweig, Stefan. *Conqueror of the Seas: The Story of Magellan.* New York: Zweig Press, 2007.

Internet Addresses

Ferdinand Magellan
<http://www.newadvent.org/cathen/09526b.htm>

Ferdinand Magellan and the First Circumnavigation of the World
<http://www.mariner.org/educationalad/ageofex/ magellan.php>
The Mariners' Museum provides an overview of this amazing explorer.

Index